bang on the door™ ©

football crazy's activity book

Collins

An imprint of HarperCollinsPublishers

Footie is my favourite thing,
They call me **football crazy**.
There's lots inside for you to do,
Get going – don't be lazy!

The team have left a great big mess,
It really isn't fair!
Can you help **football crazy**
Sort the boots out into pairs?
1
2
3
Sort the
boots into
pairs by drawing
lines to match
them up.
10
4
5
9
8
7
6

Dream Team

When **football crazy** goes to bed,
He finds he always dreams
About fantastic football games,
And all his favourite teams!

Cross out any letters that appear in the grid 3 times. The leftover letters will spell out one of the teams in **football crazy**'s dream. Who is it?

x	j	a	k	x
r	w	b	j	s
y	e	j	k	w
b	k	x	n	y
w	a	y	l	b

Goal!
He shoots, he scores!
Football crazy's super cool.
Look at all the goals he's got
The net's completely full!
How many penalties has
football crazy scored?
Count the balls
on the page.

See if you can put all of these countries correctly into the grid. We've given you 3 to start off.

NORTHERN IRELAND (15)
SCOTLAND (8)
GERMANY (7)
NORWAY (6)
ITALY (5)
CAMEROON (8)
DENMARK (7)
BRAZIL (6)
WALES (5)
SPAIN (5)
SWEDEN (6)
ENGLAND (7)
FRANCE (6)
EIRE (4)
USA (3)

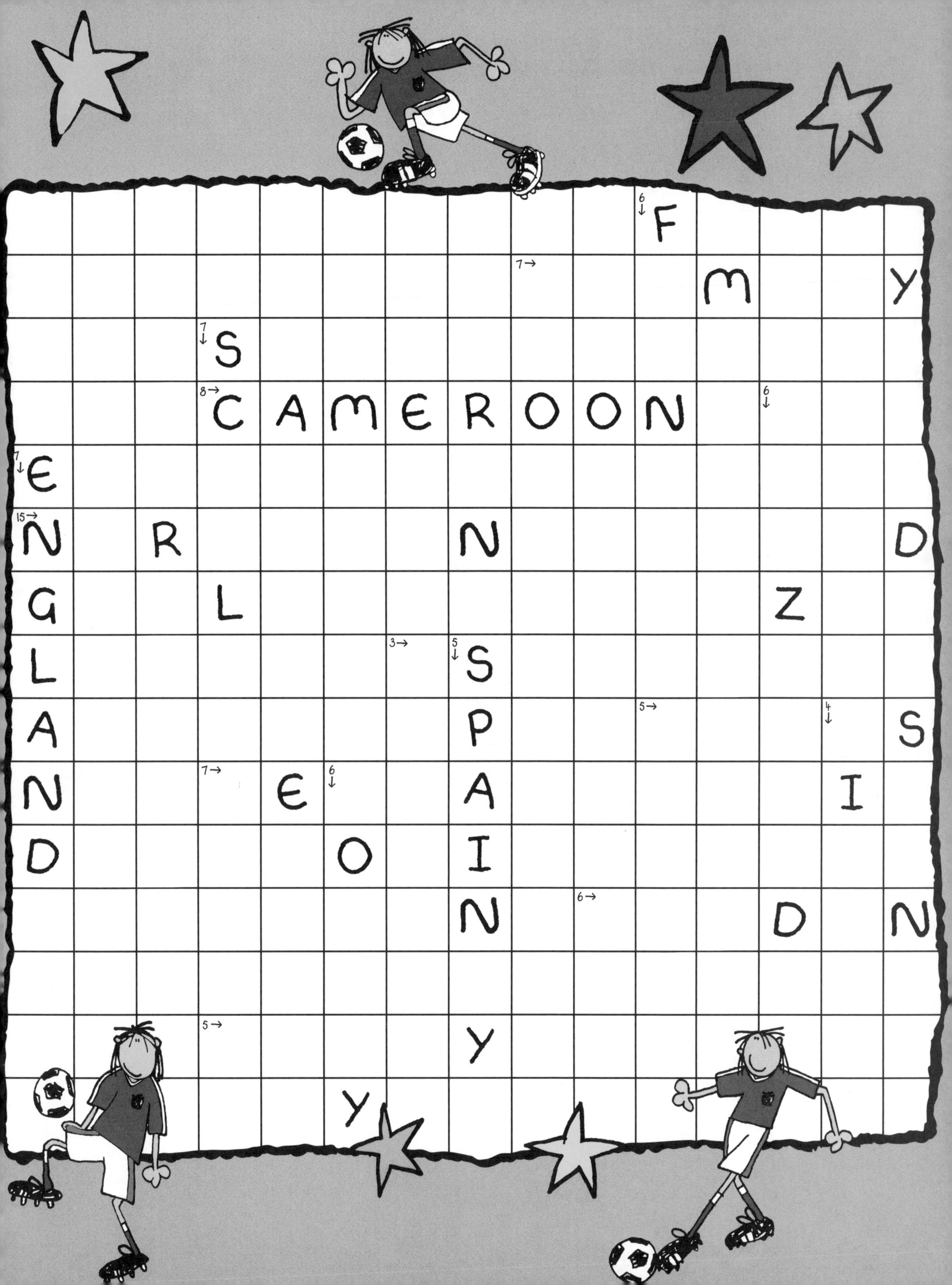
CAMEROON
ENGLAND
SPAIN

Lots and lots of goals so far,
All the teams have scored.
Can you do the sums to find
The leaders on the board?

team	away goals	home goals	points
Cupthorne City	4	3	11
Kickchester Town	5	1	....
Goals Utd	2	5	....
Bang on the Door Utd	7	6	....
Leadersville	3	4	....
Trophy Town	4	4	....
Boots City Wanderers	1	3	....
Team Rovers	6	2	....

If HOME goals score 1 point each and AWAY goals score 2, how many points does each team have? Which team are in the lead?
Winning Team
....

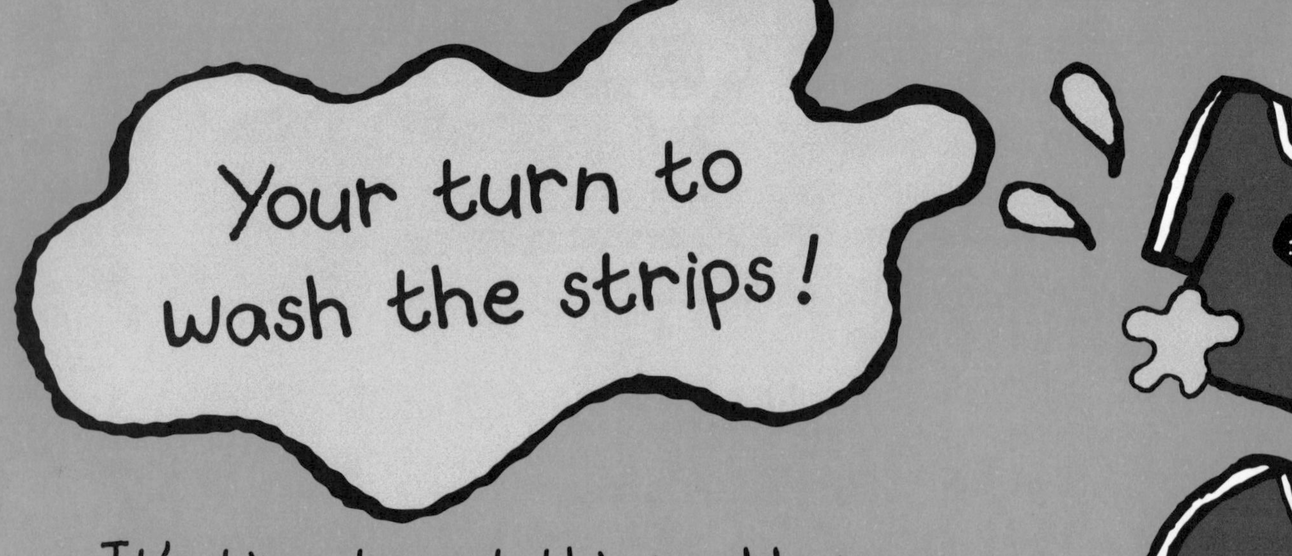

It's time to get this muddy mess
Cleared up nice and clean.
Can you sort out what is what
For each guy in the team?

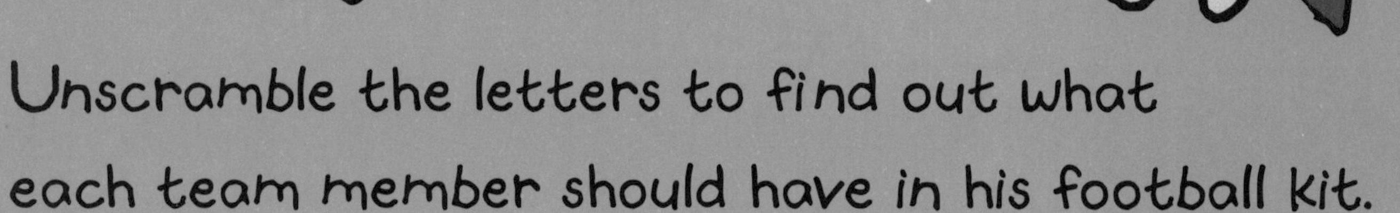

Unscramble the letters to find out what each team member should have in his football kit.

thorss _ _ _ _ _ _

sejery _ _ _ _ _ _

cosks _ _ _ _ _

sobot _ _ _ _ _

ruckistat _ _ _ _ _ _ _ _ _

There's no stopping football crazy,
He's having lots of fun.
Help him through the maze to score
And make him number one!
Entrance

Time for Training
Do you want to play this game?
Two to four take part.
Snip the counters from the page
And throw a 6 to start!
Get ready to train with this game for 2,3 or 4 players. Use your safety scissors to carefully snip off the playing pieces at the edge of the page. Throw a dice to move around the pitch and follow the commands as you go. The winner is the first to finish the training and get back to the changing rooms. You have to throw a 6 to start.
1 Start here
2
3
4 You've dribbled the ball through the cones without knocking any over. Have another go
5 You do 20 press-ups no probs! Move forward 2
6
7 You miss a penalty! Go back 1

Goal!
20
You're the fastest on the pitch and first back to the changing rooms.
You're a winner!
16
Oops! Your boot has come off.
Throw a 6 before you can move again
17
18
19
Ouch! You are sent off for a bad tackle.
Go back 4 spaces
15
14
13
You are injured in a tackle.
Miss a turn while you run it off
8
9
You are last in a sprint challenge.
Miss a turn, while you recover
10
Half-time oranges give you lots of energy.
Move forward 2 spaces
11
12

Football crazy really wants
A brand new football strip.
Why don't you design a kit
That's super cool and hip?
Design and
colour a new
strip for
football crazy!

Can you spot 8 differences between these two pictures?

These two may look just the same,
But in fact they're not.
Look really close and you will see
One changes quite a lot!

The Big Match!

Five new pairs of footie boots
Are hidden in this pic.
See if you can find them all,
Let's start looking, quick!

Hidden all around this pic
Are five pairs of footie boots.
See if you can find them all,
Come on – have a look!
love
bang on the

Football Crazy!

The whistle blows and off they go,
Running all around.
Look hard and you will see these words,
On the footie ground!

goal
league
header
whistle
corner
game
pitch
linesman
strip
football
net
players
post
trophy
penalty
team
referee

Words can read up, down, forwards, backwards or diagonally.

o l e a g u e t h
r e f e r e e r e
p e n a l t y o a
p l a y e r s p d
i e c e s h e h e
t p o s t y f y r
c e r t r g o a l
h f n g i e o o e
s x e e p t t e t
t f r i e e b e n
e s o o t g a m e
a w h i s t l e t
m d e h n e l r h
l i n e s m a n s

Result!
Yippee! The team has won again,
The boys are over the moon!
Do the quiz to count their wins,
This season's finished soon.
• Start with the number of players
on the pitch during the game (22)...
22
• Add the number of match officials (4)...
• Take away the goalies (2)...
• Divide by the number of goals
scored if the final score is 3–1 (4)...
• Multiply by the number of goals
scored in a hat-trick (3)...
• Football crazy's team have won....
games so far this season.

Player of the year!

Football crazy is the best,
He's Player of the year.
Help him pick out two the same
And then you'll hear the cheer!

Only 2 of the football boots
are exactly the same.
Which ones?

We are the champions!
The footie season's at an end
But our little lad's not sad
Join up the dots to see this prize
It's well and truly fab!
1
2
3
4
5
6
7
8
9
10
11
12
13
14
15
16
17
18
19
20
21
22
23
24
25
26
27
28
29

Answers

Sort the Boots

1 and 4 match

2 and 8 match

3 and 7 match

5 and 9 match

6 and 10 match

Dream Team

The team is **Arsenal**

Goal!

There are 17 balls

World Cup!

										F				
								G	E	R	M	A	N	Y
			S							A				
			C	A	M	E	R	O	O	N		B		
E			O							C		R		
N	O	R	T	H	E	R	N	I	R	E	L	A	N	D
G			L									Z		
L			A			U	S	A				I		
A			N				P			W	A	L	E	S
N			D	E	N	M	A	R	K				I	
D					O		I						R	
					R		N		S	W	E	D	E	N
					W									
			I	T	A	L	Y							
					Y									

Leader Board

The winning team is

Bang on the Door Utd

Your turn to wash the strips!

thors – **shorts**

sejery – **jersey**

cosks – **socks**

sobot – **boots**

ruckistat – **tracksuit**

Maze

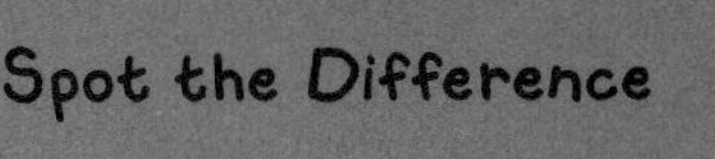

The Big Match

Football Crazy

Result!

The answer is 18

Player of the year!

1 and 8 are the same

Answers

Collect 5 tokens and get a free poster!*

All you have to do is collect five funky tokens!

You can snip one from any of these cool Bang on the Door books!

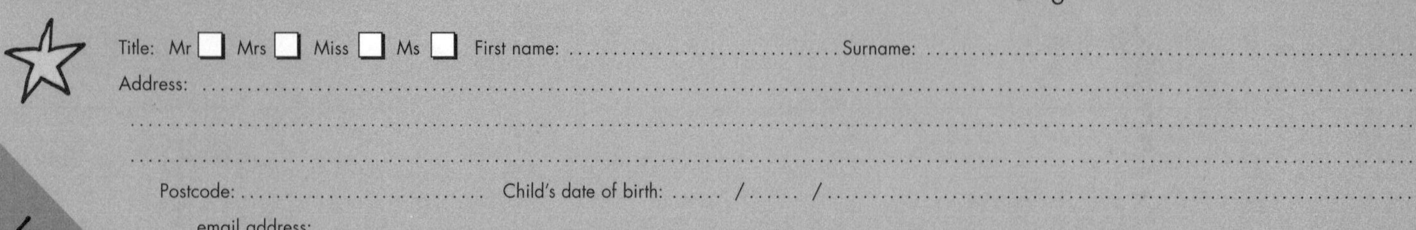

Title: Mr ☐ Mrs ☐ Miss ☐ Ms ☐ First name: .... Surname: ....

Address: ....

....

....

Postcode: .... Child's date of birth: ...... /...... /........................

email address: ....

Signature of parent/guardian: ....

Tick here if you wish to receive further information about children's books ☐

Terms and Conditions: Proof of sending cannot be considered proof of receipt. Not redeemable for cash. Please allow 28 days for delivery. Photocopied tokens not accepted. Offer open to UK, New Zealand and Australia residents only while stocks last. *rrp £3.99

FC01

1 token